AMAZING FEATS OF

ELECTRICAL ENGINEERING

Essential Library
An Imprint of Abdo Publishing | www.abdopublishing.com

ELECTRICAL ENGINEERING

by Jennifer Swanson

Content Consultant

Don Cripps
Electrical and Computer Engineering Department
Utah State University

www.abdopublishing.com

Published by Abdo Publishing, a division of ABDO, PO Box 398166, Minneapolis, Minnesota 55439. Copyright © 2015 by Abdo Consulting Group, Inc. International copyrights reserved in all countries. No part of this book may be reproduced in any form without written permission from the publisher. Essential Library™ is a trademark and logo of Abdo Publishing.

Printed in the United States of America, North Mankato, Minnesota
042014
092014

Cover Photo: US Air Force
Interior Photos: US Air Force, 2, 36, 39, 51, 55, 59; Eric Risberg/AP Images, 7; Mel Evans/AP Images, 9; Sandra Chereb/AP Images, 11; T.G. Paschal/Tuscaloosa News/AP Images, 15; Dusty Compton/Tuscaloosa News/AP Images, 17; Bettmann/Corbis, 19, 43; Alexander Blaikley/Corbis, 20; Schenectady Museum/Hall of Electrical History Foundation/Corbis, 24; Sander van der Werf/Shutterstock Images, 27; NASA, 28; Henry Burroughs/AP Images, 30; NOAA, 33; Science and Society/SuperStock, 41; Douglas C. Pizac/AP Images, 44; Anthony Bolante/Reuters/Corbis, 47; Dmitry Kalinovsky/Shutterstock Images, 49; Red Line Editorial, 54; Proehl Studios/Corbis, 57, 62; Don Ryan/AP Images, 60, 94; Peter Endig/dpa/Corbis, 64; Charles Dharapak/AP Images, 67; Dominique Leppin/epa/Corbis, 69; Paul Chinn/San Francisco Chronicle/Corbis, 71; David Paul Morris/Getty Images, 73; Kim Kulish/Corbis, 74; Mike Blake/Reuters/Corbis, 77; Car Culture/Car Culture/Corbis, 79; Rex Features/AP Images, 81; Steven Senne/AP Images, 84; Eli Lucero/The Herald Journal/AP Images, 87; Tony Avelar/Bloomberg/Getty Images, 89; HO/Reuters/Corbis, 91; Michael Sohn/AP Images, 96

Editor: Arnold Ringstad
Series Designer: Becky Daum

Library of Congress Control Number: 2014932576

Cataloging-in-Publication Data

Swanson, Jennifer.
 Amazing feats of electrical engineering / Jennifer Swanson.
   p. cm. -- (Great achievements in engineering)
Includes index.
ISBN 978-1-62403-428-2
1. Electrical engineering--Juvenile literature.   I. Title.
621--dc23

2014932576

Cover: The satellites of the global positioning system orbit Earth at an altitude of approximately 12,550 miles (20,200 km).

CONTENTS

CHAPTER 1

LICENSED TO DRIVE

Brian Torcellini, a program manager at Google, eases his car out of the company parking lot and onto the side streets of Silicon Valley, the area of California commonly considered the technology capital of the world. He is headed toward Route 101, better known as the Pacific Coast Highway, a stretch of road traveling up the California coast. To many drivers, this would be the beginning of a typical day on the road. But Torcellini's trip will be anything but typical. He is about to relinquish his driving duties to the robotic technology of Google's driverless car. The concept of a driverless car has been around for decades, mostly in movies and books. Today, with the advent of the

The technology to make driverless cars possible has become widely available only in the last few years.

Global Positioning System (GPS), street mapping, and laser sensors, the possibility of autonomous driving is becoming a reality.

Why a driverless car? Google founders Larry Page and Sergey Brin have goals far beyond the search engine technology that made Google famous. They envision technology that solves problems and improves the world. Sebastian Thrun, lead engineer of the Google driverless car project, sees the mission of the autonomous car as a way to "help prevent traffic accidents, free up people's time, and reduce carbon emissions by fundamentally changing car use."[1] Google is the first company to achieve major successes with driverless car prototypes. Torcellini's drive is yet another test of the vehicle's capabilities.

He maneuvers the car onto the on-ramp and merges smoothly into traffic on the Pacific Coast Highway. He pushes a small yellow button on a console between the front seats, and a female voice announces, "Autodriving."[2] Torcellini takes his foot off the accelerator and removes his hands from the steering wheel. The Google car independently surges forward into the crowded lanes of traffic. The car assesses its surroundings and makes minor adjustments to speed and steering. It maneuvers out of a nearby car's blind spot and avoids a truck traveling too close to it. So far, the test has been successful.

ENGINEERED DRIVING

The driverless car performs these driving tasks using a combination of laser arrays, sensors, video cameras, and radar to move itself in and out of traffic. The rotating sensor mounted on the roof scans in all directions to generate a detailed map of the car and its surroundings. Three radar sensors spread evenly across the front bumper and one sensor on the back bumper keep the car aware of its position in traffic. A video camera mounted inside the car next to the rearview mirror scans the area ahead to detect obstructions such as bicyclists, pedestrians, and even stoplights. It also tracks the lane lines on the road to ensure the car stays in the correct spot. The position estimator sensor takes rapid readings as the car makes tiny changes to its path, ensuring the vehicle stays on the correct predetermined heading.

A driver cuts in front of Torcellini's car and the autonomous system slows the vehicle immediately to avoid a collision. Anthony Levandowski, one of the lead engineers on the driverless car project, sits in the passenger seat and monitors the system on his laptop. "We adjusted our speed to give him a little room," he later recalled, "just like a person would."[3] The driverless car zooms safely along the winding roads of the Pacific Coast Highway just as it was designed to do.

Nevada governor Brian Sandovol took a ride in a Google driverless car a few weeks after the state permitted the vehicles on its roads.

DRIVER'S TEST

With more than 140,000 miles (225,000 km) logged in its driverless cars, Google was confident in the reliability of its system.[4] Still, the company needed government cooperation to obtain licenses for operating self-driving cars. Nevada was the first state to offer an official driving test to the Google driverless car. The test was crucial to the success of the program. The car had to navigate Las Vegas Boulevard, a street normally alive with thousands of people and covered in brightly colored billboards, enough to distract even the most focused of drivers. It performed flawlessly. The state of Nevada granted the Google self-driving car its own license. One significant condition is that two people must always be present in the car—one behind the wheel and one in the passenger seat. They must be prepared to take control if something goes wrong.

The success of the Google self-driving car project would not be possible without the engineers who worked on its design, creation, and implementation. Google gathered some of the best electrical, industrial, and computer engineers in the world and allocated more

EXPERIENCED ENGINEERS

The engineers of the Google car program are experienced and well respected in their field. Chris Urmson won awards for the driverless cars he worked on at Carnegie Mellon University. Software expert Mike Montemerlo has his PhD in electrical and computer engineering. Another engineer, Anthony Levandowski, once worked on a car that could deliver pizza without a driver.

than $50 million for the design, production, and creation of a workable autonomous car.[5]

Electrical engineering and computer engineering are closely related. The field of electrical engineering came into being in the 1800s, shortly after the properties of electricity were discovered and explained. Computers, developed in the 1900s, are powered by electricity. This means it is critical computer engineers understand how electricity works.

THINKING LOGICALLY

Engineers have exciting and interesting jobs that require them to approach problems systematically and logically. Specifically, electrical engineers directly affect the everyday lives of everyone who uses electricity. In the twenty-first century, this includes nearly everyone on Earth.

An electrical engineer may be called on to design radio and television transmitters, work on telephone networks, or set up electric power

EVERYDAY INNOVATION

The work of electrical engineers often impacts people's daily lives. Shadi Dayeh, a professor of electrical and computer engineering at the University of California, San Diego, has developed a way to improve the life of the batteries used in smartphones and other common devices. By coating wires within a battery with the element silicon, Dayeh was able to enhance durability and increase the life of the battery. If the 2013 development is put into practice, it may affect every person who uses a handheld electronic device.

THE VALUE OF ELECTRICAL ENGINEERS

According to the US Bureau of Labor Statistics, more than 20 percent of all employed electrical engineers work for architectural or engineering firms. The average annual salary for an electrical engineer is almost $92,000, but earnings can rise to $136,000 or more.[6] According to the executive director of the National Association of Colleges and Employers,

"Engineering majors are consistently among the highest paid because the demand for them is so great."[7] The minimum requirement for a job is typically a bachelor of science degree in electrical engineering. Obtaining a graduate degree in the field can lead to higher paying jobs and new opportunities, such as teaching the subject at a university.

distribution systems. If an object has a switch that can be turned on or off and is supplied by electricity, an electrical engineer likely aided in its design.

Engineers like to figure out how things work, apply what they have learned, and solve problems. They must be able to collaborate with other engineers to determine the best, most efficient design for a particular object or system. Electrical engineers are in-depth thinkers who appreciate the challenges of analyzing and solving complicated problems using logical thinking. However, engineering is much more than

Solar panels are one of today's most popular areas of electrical engineering research and development.

just charts, graphs, diagrams, and numbers. Engineers think creatively, developing objects and systems the world has never seen before.

CHAPTER 2

ELECTRICAL ENGINEERING

Electrical engineering is one of many different types of engineering. In general, the field deals with designing, developing, and testing electronic equipment. The field of electrical engineering touches almost every aspect of modern-day life in some way.

Electrical engineers work in a wide range of disciplines. Some design the cell phones we use every day. Others create navigation systems for ships at sea. Some engineers work to upgrade the computer networks that make up the Internet. Others design and maintain the power

Electrical engineers have been at the forefront of cutting-edge technology since the profession began more than a century ago.

plants that supply the modern world with electricity. To keep up with the rapid pace of today's technological advances, electrical engineers use innovative techniques and tools to stay on the cutting edge.

ENGINEERS AND ELECTRICITY

Engineering is the process of identifying problems and designing solutions. If people need to cross a body of water, engineers design a bridge. If many people need to live in a small area of land, engineers design a tall building. If people need to travel long distances, engineers design a road. As the presence of ancient bridges, buildings, and roads attests, engineering has existed for thousands of years. However, human beings have learned how to tame electricity much more recently. While natural electricity sources such as lightning, static electricity, and electrified animals were known, little was understood about how electricity actually worked. People began understanding this mysterious form of energy through its connection with another force: magnetism.

Like electricity, magnetism had been long known but little understood. More than 2,000 years ago, sailors began using pieces of magnetic rock called lodestones to navigate the seas. When floated in a bowl of water, the lodestone would always point south. The reasons for this were finally identified and outlined in astronomer William Gilbert's scientific paper

De Magnete, published in 1600. Gilbert, sometimes known as the father of electrical engineering, was the first scientist to theorize Earth itself is a great magnet. He called the force between two objects *electrick* force.

Gilbert helped pioneer the study of magnetism, but he failed to make the connection between it and electricity.

Faraday was well known for lecturing on his discoveries to his peers and the general public.

In the 1800s, Michael Faraday took Gilbert's initial findings and expanded them dramatically by proving a connection between electricity and magnetism. He showed how the movement of a magnet inside a coil of wire could produce electricity. His theory led to the concept of electromagnetism, the interaction between electricity and magnetic fields. His work also led to the invention of the first electric motor. Faraday experimented with his motor to determine how he could transmit electricity on a grand scale. Faraday eventually created the first electric generator, a simple dynamo, as a means to supply steady electric power.

CIRCUITS, VOLTAGE, AND CURRENT

Electrical engineers are schooled in the basics of electricity. A circuit is simply a closed loop through which flows a steady stream of subatomic particles known as electrons. The flow of electrons, called a current, can carry energy from place to place. A basic electric circuit might consist of a battery connected by two wires to a light bulb. When the wires are attached to both the battery and the bulb, the loop is closed and current flows. The electrons require a push known as voltage to move along the wire. This push often comes from a source of power, such as a battery. The push is measured in volts. The rate at which the flow happens is known as amperage, measured in amps. The total power is equal to the voltage multiplied by the amperage. Power is commonly measured in watts.

Dynamos take advantage of the relationship between electricity and magnetism. When a wire rotates within a magnetic field, it generates electricity. Faraday's designs are the basis for many power generation systems today.

TAMING ELECTRICITY

Faraday's achievements inspired others to delve into electricity and its relationship with magnetism. This eventually led to new ideas and scientific laws describing the phenomena. But it was Scottish scientist James Clerk Maxwell, perhaps one of the greatest scientific minds of the 1800s, who took Faraday's idea of electromagnetism and gave it a mathematical foundation. Maxwell determined the mathematical equations that describe how electric and magnetic fields spread and interact.

In the late 1800s, engineer Oliver Heaviside condensed Maxwell's equations into more usable forms. He took Maxwell's theories and applied them to the distortion encountered when sending signals along telegraph or telephone lines. Because different parts of signals travel at different speeds, long-distance lines suffered from distortion. Heaviside showed mathematically how changes could be made to the line's design to avoid the distortion problem. This development paved the way for future technologies that transmitted signals over wires. Heaviside was recognized as a pioneer in the field of electrical engineering and was awarded the prestigious Faraday Medal by the Institute of Electrical Engineers in the United Kingdom, now called the Institution of Engineering and Technology.

German physicist Heinrich Hertz and Italian engineer Guglielmo Marconi developed a new field for electrical engineering in the late 1800s: the wireless transmission of signals, also known as radio. Hertz proved electromagnetic waves existed, validating a prediction made by Maxwell. The scientific unit of frequency, hertz, was later named after him. Marconi

RADIO BANDS AND FREQUENCIES

When engineers work with signals that are transmitted through the air, they need to be aware of the radio band or frequency they are using. Signals sent as radio frequencies (RF) are electromagnetic waves. Along with X rays and visible light, they form part of the electromagnetic spectrum. Radio transmissions are the basis for wireless communication systems, including those used in satellites. Each RF signal has a wavelength, amplitude, and frequency. The distance between waves is the wavelength. The height of the waves is the amplitude. The number of waves sent in a particular time period is the frequency. Altering these variables makes it possible for radio waves to carry information. AM radio waves have their amplitude changed, while FM radio waves have their frequency changed. Bands, or groups of frequencies, are established so different types of communication do not overlap.

helped create practical uses for sending and receiving signals using these waves. His achievements include the first wireless radio signal sent over the Atlantic Ocean.

ELECTRICAL ENGINEERING TODAY

The Massachusetts Institute of Technology (MIT) and Cornell University were among the first universities in the United States to offer an undergraduate degree in electrical engineering. The courses for the electrical engineering major were initially associated with physics

departments, but in the early 1900s each university established its own engineering department and moved the electrical engineering major there.

The skills developed by electrical engineers cross over into many different engineering disciplines. For example, the aerospace engineers who design airplanes and rockets rely on electrical engineering to create the systems that let pilots and astronauts communicate and navigate. The most prominent crossover point is in the area of computer engineering. With the invention of the computer in the 1900s, electrical technology has exploded. Electrical engineering is so deeply linked to computer engineering that many modern colleges and universities combine both areas into one department.

Today at MIT, the electrical engineering department is combined with computer engineering and accounts for more than 20 percent of the school's graduates.[1] The fast-paced advances in electrical engineering and computers continue to make the field popular. Today's engineers design and test electrical equipment ranging from orbiting satellites to power plants to robots. If something uses electricity to function, an electrical engineer likely played a part in designing it.

CHAPTER 3

CREATING GPS

Electrical engineering is all about designing the systems that make up our modern high-tech world. These include satellite navigation, energy production, and communication systems. The first of these, satellite navigation, has entered into widespread use only in the last few decades. GPS has changed the way ordinary people navigate through their streets, cities, and countries. At the same time, it serves vital purposes for soldiers on the battlefield, sailors at sea, and pilots in the sky. The concept of GPS originated in the late 1950s, when the United States and the Soviet Union competed to make advances in space technology. The competition was known as the space race.

For many people, GPS devices have completely replaced the paper maps that were standard for centuries.

The best-known results of the space race were the US landings on the moon, but satellite technology was also critically important. The electrical engineers who created the satellites of the 1950s and 1960s paved the way for GPS technology. This navigation system has become so commonplace it is hard to imagine life without it.

THE SPACE RACE

The 1950s marked the beginning of the Cold War between the communist Soviet Union and the democratic United States. After cooperating during World War II (1939–1945), both countries longed to display the superiority of their own society and form of government. The space race was one of many arenas in which the two powerful nations competed. They sought

The success of *Explorer 1* laid the groundwork not just for further space exploration, but also for GPS.

to demonstrate their scientific and engineering prowess by launching rockets to explore space. The Soviets succeeded in launching the first artificial satellite, *Sputnik*, in October 1957. The space race suddenly heated up.

The United States launched its own satellite, *Explorer 1*, in January 1958. It contained a control system to guide the satellite to the proper orbit, scientific instruments to gather data about space, and a communication system to relay this data back to Earth. Soon, both nations were launching many satellites.

Scientists wanted to be able to track the large number of satellites being launched. The US Navy turned to Roger Easton to build the world's first satellite tracking system. Easton, a research physicist working at the Naval Research Laboratory, collaborated with electrical engineer Milton Rosen to develop Minitrack, a satellite tracking system capable of pinpointing the position of a satellite flying overhead.

FROM MINITRACK TO GPS

To determine the accurate position of a satellite in space, the engineers built six monitoring stations situated along the same line of longitude. The line passed through Canada, New York State, Peru, Chile, and Antarctica. Each station used antennae to record when satellites passed over it. The

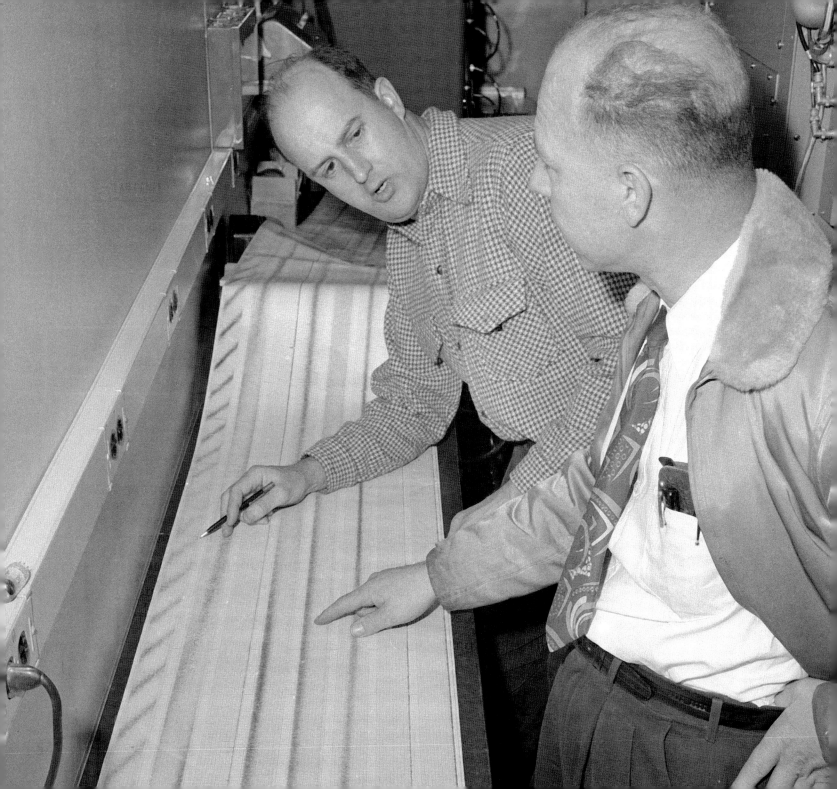

stations then transmitted the information to other monitoring stations. Comparing the timing of satellite passes over the fixed locations of the stations made it possible to determine exactly how far away from the stations the satellites were. This provided the precise positions of the satellites in space.

The GPS system, also developed by Easton, works in a similar way but in reverse. A collection of GPS satellites orbits the Earth. They are placed into many different orbits so multiple satellites are visible from any point on the planet's surface at any given time. A GPS device on the surface receives a signal from the satellites overhead. The signal tells where the satellite is located at that instant. By analyzing the locations of the satellites it sees, a GPS device can determine its exact position on the planet's surface. This concept was tested on Navigation Technology Satellite 2 (NTS-2), launched by the United States in 1977. The satellite included precise clocks, antennae to communicate with Earth, and solar panels to provide electricity. NTS-2 worked, clearing the way for the widespread deployment of GPS satellites.

Electrical engineers play a part in all areas of GPS construction and maintenance. They develop the mathematical equations and calculations, known as algorithms, that GPS devices use to calculate a location.

Electrical engineers also practice systems engineering, a discipline that studies complicated engineering projects over the entire life cycle of their development and use. This is an important concept to use when working on GPS. Old satellites are frequently retired and new satellites are launched. Satellites more than 20 years old must function alongside brand-new ones, meaning engineers must control how the many different parts of GPS work together.

HOW A GPS SATELLITE WORKS

Today's GPS includes 24 satellites in orbit approximately 12,550 miles (20,200 km) above Earth.[1] At this altitude, each one travels around Earth twice per day. The satellites transmit ultrahigh frequency (UHF) signals containing precise time and position data. The signals are then picked up by GPS devices on Earth, including airplane navigation equipment, military targeting systems, and even common smartphones.

GPS satellites require three separate components to function properly: a communication system, a power source, and a control system. The communication portion consists of an antenna capable of sending and receiving radio signals from command centers on Earth. The power source on a satellite typically comes from batteries and solar panels. Energy from

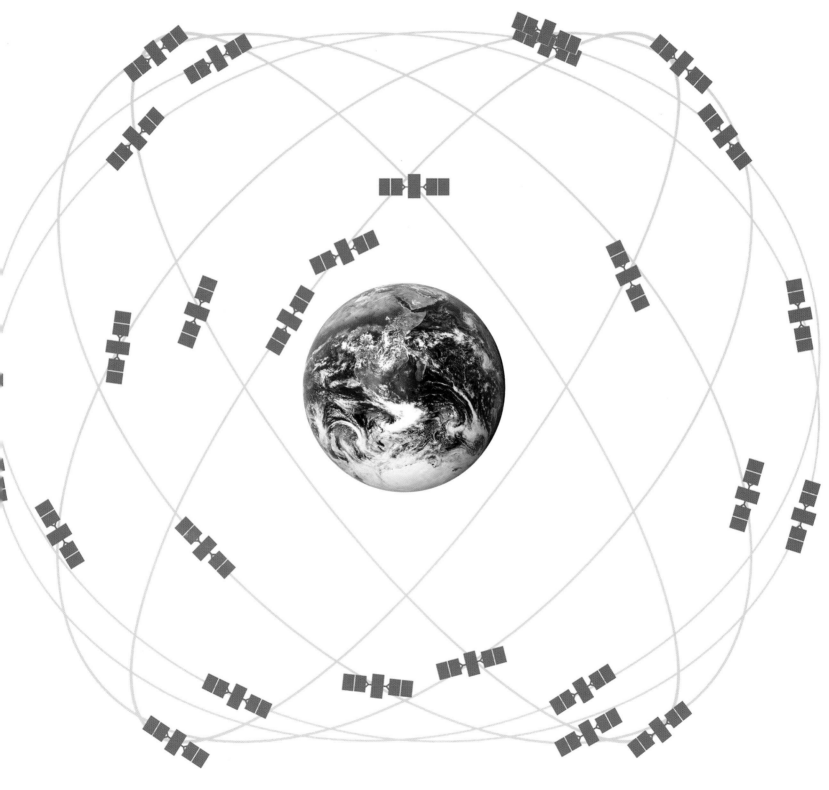

ENGINEERING AND SCIENCE

In 1915, Albert Einstein developed the special theory of relativity. The physics and math behind his theory are complicated, but the key point it makes is that the speed of light is always exactly the same. One effect predicted by the theory is called time dilation, which says objects moving quickly experience a slower passage of time than slower objects. The difference is very small at normal human speeds, but it is significant enough that engineers had to take it into account when designing the GPS satellites. The satellites move so quickly that their clocks tick approximately seven microseconds more slowly each day than clocks on Earth. Over time, this can change GPS calculations enough to give inaccurate location readings. Engineers designed the satellites to take the difference into account. The satellites provide an important example of the connection between scientific discoveries and engineering.

the sun is collected by a solar panel and channeled to a battery to keep the satellite running.

The control system of a GPS satellite involves onboard computers that work together with command centers on the ground. They determine where to maneuver and what information to send back to Earth. The system also includes extremely accurate clocks that provide timing information that is transmitted to the ground.

MANEUVERING A GPS SATELLITE

Satellites are assigned specific locations in space called orbital slots. Shifting a satellite's position from its designated orbital slot can cause signal disruptions on the ground or inaccurate location data. It can even cause the satellite's orbit to decay, circling Earth closer and closer until the satellite burns up in the atmosphere. Since GPS satellites must provide precise location and timing data to calculate position, it is critical each satellite maintains a precise orbital slot.

Movement of a satellite in space is achieved through attitude control systems and onboard propulsion systems. Attitude control keeps the satellite pointed at the proper angle to send data to receivers on the ground. This is accomplished through devices called reaction wheels. Inside the satellite, motors turn a set of wheels at a set rate. The spinning motion of the wheels keeps the satellite stable. When engineers need to turn a satellite in place, they vary the speed of one or more of the wheels, resulting in a precise

STUDENTS IN ACTION

Students at Cornell University studying electrical engineering can become members of the school's Global Positioning System Laboratory. The lab develops algorithms to prevent GPS signals from interference, also known as jamming. It also designs new satellites to improve the reliability and dependability of GPS data in the harsh conditions of space.

35

movement in the desired direction. Reaction wheels can only rotate a satellite in place. They cannot move the satellite to a new orbit. For that, a satellite relies on onboard propulsion systems consisting of thruster rockets. Powered by chemical fuel, thrusters push the satellite through space and keep it in the proper orbital slot.

Electrical engineers work on all aspects of GPS, from designing transmitters and clocks to improving the reliability of the satellites' electronics to developing equipment that can survive in the harsh environment of space. They also design, construct, and test GPS receivers and create algorithms to determine position using GPS signals. Engineers trained in computer science develop hardware and software for use in practical applications of GPS, such as in cellular phones or car navigation systems.

CHAPTER 4

GPS IN ACTION

The primary goal of GPS is to provide its users with accurate position, navigation, and timing information consistently and quickly. GPS provides one of two types of location information, depending on who is using it. The US military has access to the precise positioning service (PPS), while civilians can use only the standard positioning service (SPS).

Initially, the US government allowed only the military to use accurate GPS data. The SPS included built-in errors that greatly reduced the accuracy of the location data it provided compared with PPS. This

The reliability of GPS depends on the US Air Force personnel who operate and maintain the satellites.

COMPONENTS OF A GPS SIGNAL

Each GPS signal transmitted to Earth has three specific pieces of information: the ephemeris data, a pseudorandom code, and almanac data. The ephemeris data includes timing information. It also tells whether the satellite is operating properly. The pseudorandom code is an identification code assigned to a specific satellite. It is used so that a receiver can tell which satellite is transmitting. The almanac data includes information on where the satellite is located.

changed when President Bill Clinton ordered accurate GPS signals be made available to the public starting in 2000. As a result, worldwide use of GPS technology exploded. GPS is now found in boats, cars, planes, and even personal cell phones. PPS still provides more precise location data, but SPS is accurate enough for everyday applications. Typically, SPS is accurate to within a few meters, while PPS can be accurate to within a few centimeters.

RECEIVING DATA

The signals from GPS satellites are captured by GPS receiver antennas situated at 16 worldwide monitoring stations. The stations are crewed by teams of engineers who track the satellites as they fly overhead and transmit signals. Engineers ensure the satellites and receivers are operating correctly.

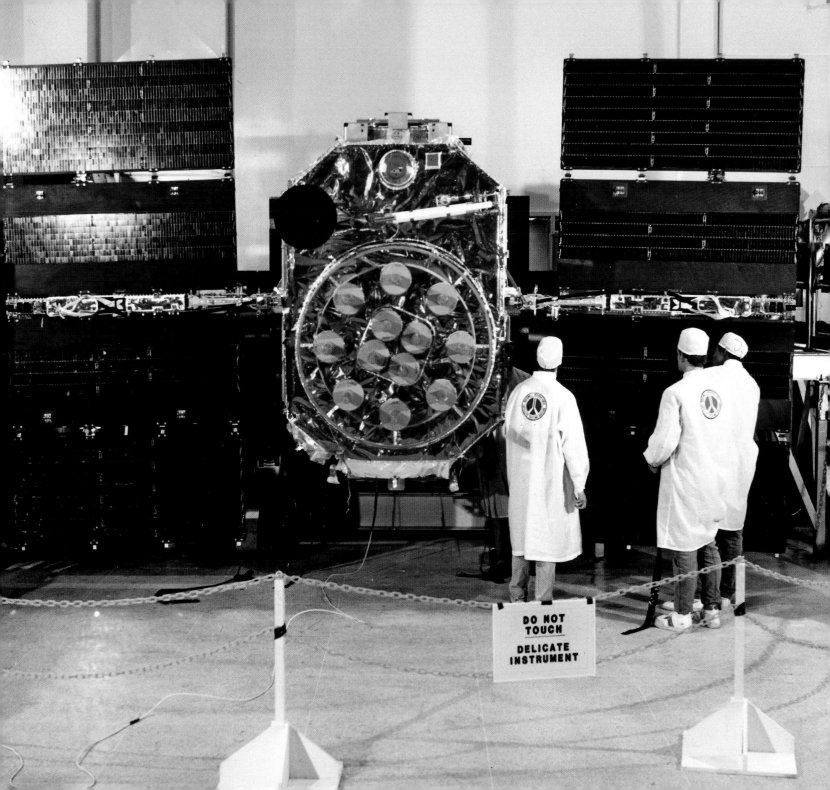

DO NOT
TOUCH

DELICATE
INSTRUMENT

CALCULATING A POSITION

A GPS receiver compares the time a signal was sent with the time it was received. It knows the signal travels at the speed of light, so it can use the difference in time to calculate the distance of the receiver from the satellite. The receiver tracks this data from multiple satellites at once to establish its exact location.

Each GPS satellite contains precise atomic clocks. These devices rely on the steady behavior of cesium or rubidium atoms rather than the ticking of a clock mechanism. This makes it possible to make the clocks amazingly accurate. Someone observing one of these clocks would have to view it for approximately 32,000 years for its accuracy to be off by one second.[1] Despite the accuracy of the clocks, computers must still make slight adjustments to the satellites' timing data. This is due to Albert Einstein's theory of special relativity, which says that fast-moving objects experience time more slowly.

Calculating precise positions using GPS signals requires knowledge of the exact time it takes for the signal to travel from the satellite to the receiver. To obtain an accurate location, data must be collected from at least three GPS satellites. If a signal from a fourth satellite is present, the location can be determined more accurately.

Location is not the only service provided by GPS. As a side benefit, the extremely precise timing information required to generate accurate location data can also be useful in its own right. Free access to public GPS signals means that businesses can use GPS timing rather than purchasing their own expensive atomic clocks. The incredible accuracy of GPS clocks means transactions and other records can be tracked precisely.

The first atomic clock was built in 1949.

The transactions can be stored and sorted based on the GPS time they are completed.

PROBLEMS WITH GPS

With such a complicated system, there are bound to be errors. Electrical engineers combat issues with GPS, working to ensure the system remains accurate for its hundreds of millions of users.

Multiple factors may affect the accuracy of GPS and distort its time and location data. Though it travels at the speed of light, GPS data takes time to travel through the atmosphere to users on the surface. Although algorithms have been developed to account for this tiny delay, sometimes it can lead to inaccuracies in the GPS data. GPS signals are unable to pass through objects such as buildings, rocks, mountains, and even dense foliage. The signal may bounce off these objects, increasing the time it takes the signal to arrive at the receiver. Engineers take these issues into account when designing equipment to process the signals, but it is impossible to plan for every potential source of error.

To combat these problems and increase accuracy, the US government has developed various systems to improve GPS data. The Wide Area Augmentation System (WAAS) is operated by the Federal Aviation

Administration (FAA). Ordinary GPS signals do not meet FAA regulations for aircraft navigation accuracy; the WAAS enhances them. It uses permanent stations on the ground to receive GPS signals. Since the location of these stations is known, they are able to generate a corrected, more accurate version of the signal they receive. The stations pass this signal to special WAAS satellites that send the signals to receivers on board aircraft.

Another tool used to improve GPS service for pilots is called GPS Receiver Autonomous Integrity Monitoring (RAIM). The system helps pilots predict what the GPS signal quality will be throughout an upcoming flight. Electrical engineer Karen VanDyke led development of the RAIM system.

One man-made problem facing GPS accuracy is the presence of GPS jammers. These devices send out signals that interfere with those used by the satellites. The satellite signals are relatively easy to disrupt. As expert Bob Cockshott notes, "The problem is that the signal from the satellites is extremely weak—it's the equivalent of picking up the light output of a 25-watt bulb on the satellite."[2] It does not take much power to interfere with such a weak signal. As a result of this threat, the US government has cracked down on the use and installation of GPS jammers. A person possessing one can be fined up to $100,000 or more.[3]

KAREN VANDYKE

Karen VanDyke is a member of the staff at the Center for Navigation at the US Department of Transportation. She received her degrees in electrical engineering from the University of Massachusetts at Lowell.

She led the team that designed, developed, and implemented GPS RAIM systems for both the US Air Force and the FAA. She later joined the FAA to create prediction models for the GPS Wide Area and Local Area Augmentation Systems.

VanDyke believes that while GPS has come a long way, there is still much that can be done to improve it: "Legislation has brought [GPS] into our cell phones. The world's banks rely on it to time stamp their transactions. Eventually, coordinates will be part of every product and process in our lives—but first GPS must be improved and integrated with other technologies in order to achieve accurate positioning, navigation, and timing (PNT) information anytime and anywhere."[4]

VanDyke's work has made the GPS receivers in modern jets, such as the Boeing 787, as accurate as possible.

CHAPTER 5

HARNESSING THE SUN'S ENERGY

For more than a century, fossil fuels such as oil and coal have been the primary source of energy for human civilizations. However, these sources are limited. Eventually, they will run out or be so hard to extract from the ground they will not be worth the expense. Fossil fuels also pollute the atmosphere when burned, contributing to the problem of climate change. In recent years, the search for renewable energy sources that do not pollute has generated interest in solar power. Today's electrical engineers use their skills to devise more efficient and cost-effective ways of producing solar power.

Using solar panels to obtain electricity from the sun is one way to reduce reliance on Earth's limited fossil fuel resources.

WHY SOLAR?

Solar power is one of the largest untapped sources of energy on Earth. More than 173,000 trillion watts of energy strike the Earth at all times in the form of sunlight. That is enough to provide more than 10,000 times the planet's power use.[3] Even harnessing a tiny fraction of that energy could reduce reliance on polluting sources of energy such as oil and coal.

In 2007, at Nellis Air Force Base (AFB) near Las Vegas, Nevada, the culmination of years of study on solar energy became a reality. The US Air Force, along with solar energy company SunPower, opened a solar power plant with more than 70,000 panels. It is the largest plant of its type in North America, delivering 14 megawatts of power to approximately 13,200 homes on a daily basis.[1] The plant provides more than 25 percent of the total energy needed by the base's residents. According to the US Air Force, the plant is designed to be "at the forefront of federally-mandated energy conservation and renewable energy initiatives." The impact on pollution emissions will be "equivalent to planting 260,000 trees or removing 185,000 cars from the roadways."[2]

HOW SOLAR PANELS WORK

The goal of solar power is to harness light energy from the sun's rays and convert it to electricity that can be used to power homes, businesses, and even cars. The science of solar power is known as photovoltaics.

Nellis's huge solar power plant required three years of planning and 26 weeks of construction.

A photovoltaic cell is made up of several semiconductors, materials that allow electricity to flow under specific circumstances. The semiconductor material most commonly used in solar panels like the ones at Nellis is composed of silicon and either boron or phosphorous. When sunlight shines on the cell, a part of the light energy is transferred to

51

Electrical engineering students at San Diego State University enjoy a hands-on approach to learning by installing their own photovoltaic panels on top of a research trailer. They are collaborating with a California solar power company to learn how photovoltaic technology works. Both parties benefit: the students learn valuable skills for the energy careers of the future, and the company cultivates skilled, knowledgeable workers to fill those careers.

the semiconductor. The energy from the sun pushes electrons out of the silicon, enabling them to flow easily throughout the material. When devices called electrodes contact the cell, a circuit is created and current flows from the solar cell. The electrodes absorb the energy and convert it to usable electricity.

Solar arrays consist of multiple photovoltaic cells wired together. For Nellis, SunPower created two different sizes of arrays. One type has 128 cells and the other has 96 cells.[4] The larger the surface area of a solar array, the more energy is typically produced.

POWER PRODUCTION

One challenge of using solar power is that photovoltaic cells produce electricity as direct current (DC). In DC, electrons flow in a single, steady stream along a wire. DC works well for powering cars or storing energy in a battery, but homes typically receive alternating current

(AC). In AC, the flow of electrons moves like a wave that reverses direction several times per second. AC is more efficient when transporting power for long distances, such as from a power plant to a home. Engineers have designed power converters to change DC from solar panels into AC current for transportation to individual users.

The solar array at Nellis is grid connected, meaning the solar array operates alongside the base's existing power utility, the Nevada Power Company. The DC power produced by the cells is fed into a power converter where it is transformed into AC power consistent with the voltage and power needs of the utility power system. From the converter, the AC travels through a distribution system that controls when and how much of the solar-produced energy enters the utility's power lines. Loads, or objects that use electricity, can be attached to the distribution system. This allows them to receive power directly from the solar array, independently of the utility. Alternately, the power from the solar panels can be turned off and the load can receive power directly from the utility system.

TRACKING THE SUN

The movement of the sun presents another challenge for solar panels. People who have solar panels mounted on the roof of their homes often

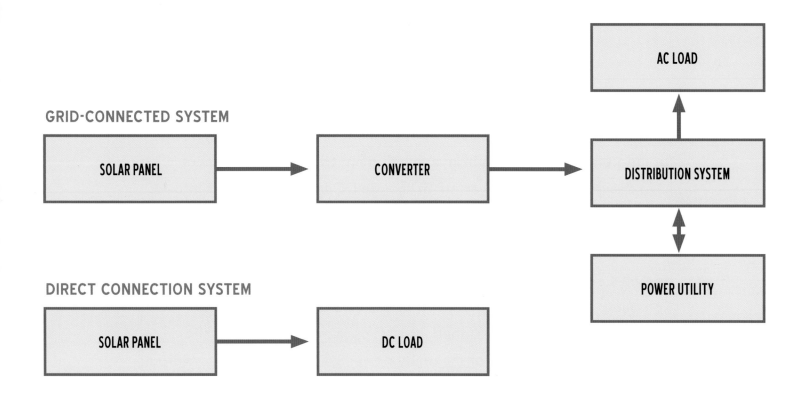

GRID-CONNECTED SYSTEM

| SOLAR PANEL | → | CONVERTER | → | DISTRIBUTION SYSTEM |

AC LOAD

POWER UTILITY

DIRECT CONNECTION SYSTEM

| SOLAR PANEL | → | DC LOAD |

A grid-connected system provides more flexibility than a system in which the solar panels are directly connected to loads.

have simple stationary panels. The amount of electricity they generate varies throughout the day, depending on the angle at which the sun strikes them. But for large solar power plants, engineers seek to maximize the amount of power generated. Tracking systems move the solar panels to maintain the optimum electricity-generating angle. This is the approach engineers took at Nellis.

The panels are supported by steel posts resting on precast concrete slabs situated at a tilt angle of 20 degrees. Engineers at SunPower developed a tracking system known as T20 to take full advantage of light

The solar panels at Nellis tilt to track the sun, increasing the amount of electricity they generate.

OPPORTUNITIES IN SOLAR POWER

According to the Solar Foundation, the number of jobs in the solar industry increased 13.2 percent between 2011 and 2012, compared with an overall job growth rate of just 2.3 percent.[5] Nearly half of all solar power companies expect to add a significant number of jobs in the next few years. For electrical engineers interested in solar power, this means they will have the opportunity to design and oversee the installation of cutting-edge photovoltaic systems.

energy from the sun. The system allows the solar arrays to be adjusted through a 45-degree angle in either direction.

Engineers designed the T20 trackers by first creating a tracking algorithm. The algorithm takes into account the time of day, time of year, and exact location of the panels to ensure they are facing the right angle at the right time. The system also detects high winds and moves the panels to a protected position if there is danger of damage. Devices called actuators move the panels back and forth when directed. The actuators require electricity to function, but this energy usage is more than offset by the power gains from efficient solar tracking. Finally, a remote network-monitoring station allows engineers to direct and control the entire system.

Similar to many other engineers today, electrical engineers are applying their knowledge and skills toward environmentally

The increasing demand for solar power plants, including the one at Nellis AFB, also generates jobs for construction workers.

friendly projects, including clean energy. Renewable energy sources are gaining favor with businesses and governments seeking an efficient, clean way of meeting their energy needs. The Nellis AFB solar plant is one of many solar plants being created to decrease reliance on scarce fossil fuels.

CHAPTER 6

SOLAR CHALLENGES

The work of engineers does not stop when a product is designed and built. Engineers must apply their skills to tackle problems that arise during the operation of a new design. The solutions should be economical in addition to being effective. The Nellis solar plant is not immune to the problems facing many solar plants in use today.

The Nellis solar plant is a grid-tie system, meaning it does not possess a backup battery. Rather than storing the electricity it generates for use at night or during cloudy conditions, the base simply switches to

Base officials flipped the switch to turn on the Nellis solar plant on December 17, 2007.

Grid-tie systems are also popular for smaller installations, such as solar-powered electric car charging stations.

the normal electric utility, Nevada Energy, during these times. The plant was built in this manner because a grid-tie system is the simplest and least expensive method of incorporating a new solar system into an existing power utility. The problem with this design is that if the utility fails, the solar panels are switched off and cannot generate power.

The utility's reasoning is that if its power goes out, it does not want electricity from solar sources flowing through power lines as workers are trying to conduct repairs.

The limitations of the Nellis AFB grid-tie system affect the energy security of the base. In a broad sense, energy security is a nation's ability to access the energy resources it needs. In this case, it refers to the base's ability to continue operating when the commercial power utility fails. The inability to use solar energy in the absence of commercial power is a serious drawback. As renewable energy consultant Scott Sklar puts it, "It's not energy security if you've got renewable generation that you cannot access if the grid goes down."[1]

One solution is to have engineers design a switch that would allow Nellis to disconnect itself from the utility grid and operate independently as needed. This would allow the solar power cells to send energy directly to the base, augmenting the power produced by the diesel backup generators already in place. The problem with this is that Nevada Energy, similar to most power utilities, charges an expensive disconnect fee for letting customers temporarily remove themselves from the utility's grid.

Another option for Nellis might be using a battery-based grid-tie system. This system sends some of the energy produced to batteries

Workers at Nellis must regularly clean the solar panels to prevent dust accumulation from reducing the panels' efficiency.

for storage and later use. If the utility goes down, the system turns on and the power from the batteries will take over the load from the base. The drawback of using batteries is that efficiency drops. Moving the electricity between the solar panels, the batteries, and the devices that require power results in energy losses. Therefore, battery power is usually only used for short periods of time during emergencies. The cost of maintaining a backup battery is also expensive, and the batteries are costly to replace when they wear out.

PHOTOVOLTAIC EFFICIENCY

A key challenge faced by electrical engineers working with solar energy is efficiency. The efficiency rate of a solar cell is the percentage of usable electricity generated from the total energy that hits the cell. The efficiency rate for most solar panels is approximately 15 percent.[2] The SunPower solar cells used at Nellis are 24 percent efficient.[3] Engineers achieved this through several design decisions. They designed the solar cells to be seamless, meaning their metal gridlines do not cover the sun-facing side of the cell. This allows the sun's rays to strike a greater surface area. There is also a mirror surface within the panel that reflects more sunlight onto the cell surface.

Electrical engineers are currently working on more ways to increase efficiency. Filbert Bartoli,

NEW USE FOR BATTERIES

The rapidly increasing use of solar energy in California has led to a new use for the batteries that power companies use to store energy. In the past, they have used batteries to store power generated at night by fossil fuel sources. Then, in the late afternoon, when people arrive home from work and electricity demand rises, the batteries' energy is put into the grid. A new plan calls for using the batteries to store the electricity generated by solar panels in the afternoon, when sunlight is strongest. Then the batteries will release power into the grid in the evening, when the sun sets.

professor of electrical and computer engineering at Lehigh University, is one of many researching organic solar cell construction. Organic photovoltaic cells (OPVs) are carbon-based polymers, or long chains of organic molecules strung together. OPVs look similar to traditional cells, but they are smaller. This means more can be placed in a given area. However, they are not as conductive and provide less than 10 percent efficiency. The potential for improvement exists, and continued research by electrical engineering departments across the world is working toward a breakthrough in OPVs. As Qiaoqiang Gan, an assistant professor of electrical engineering at the University of Buffalo, states, "Compared with their inorganic counterparts, organic photovoltaics can be fabricated over large areas on rigid or flexible substrates, potentially becoming as inexpensive as paint."[4]

INCREASING EFFICIENCY

Stephen Chou, a professor of electrical engineering at Princeton University, has developed a new organic solar cell that is able to make use of more sunlight than previous cells. He uses microscopic layers of metal and plastic to trap light in the cell and increase efficiency. The result is significantly more efficient than traditional photovoltaic cells.

COSTS OF SOLAR POWER

The major drawback of solar power, and a key reason why it has not become more popular, is its high initial cost. Installation of a solar power plant can be extremely expensive. In fact, when Steven Dumont, Air Combat Command energy manager at Nellis, was first approached to build the solar plant, he declined. He knew the cost of energy from a photovoltaic system would be approximately twenty-five cents per kilowatt-hour, much higher than the seven cents per kilowatt-hour they were paying for commercial electrical power.[5] The deciding factor was the ability to offset construction fees with federal tax credits and Nevada's renewable energy credits. Similar government programs exist across the world to encourage the development of clean energy.

The $100 million plant was constructed through a partnership with solar energy companies and the local utility.[6] The base does not own the solar arrays, but instead leases the land to SunPower and purchases the energy from them at a fixed price. The arrangement has saved Nellis approximately $1 million per year in energy costs.[7] The success of the plant at Nellis may lead to the expanded use of renewable resources at other military bases and government sites.

CHAPTER 7

A ROBOT DRIVER

Today, electrical engineers are working on projects that would have seemed like science fiction just a few decades ago: cars that can safely drive themselves. Soon, the idea of driving a car without at least some assistance from a computer may seem equally odd. With the advent of smaller, smarter computers and advanced sensors, driverless cars are becoming a reality. Google has turned its attention toward accelerating the development of robotic cars.

Google is not the first company to attempt to construct a driverless car. Many car manufacturers have their own engineers attacking the

Self-driving cars are now undergoing testing on real roads across the world.

CARS COMMUNICATING WITH EACH OTHER

According to the National Transportation Safety Board (NTSB), all cars should eventually have the ability to communicate with one another about their locations. The NTSB believes car-to-car communication may help avoid accidents and provide a greater level of safety at intersections and during lane changes. It may also help prevent rear-end accidents involving vehicles stopped at intersections.

problem. They have already developed technologies that make it possible for computers to assist drivers in small ways. Cars have long featured a system called cruise control, in which a computer controls the accelerator pedal to maintain a set speed, reducing driver fatigue on long, flat stretches of road. More recently, manufacturers have equipped cars with systems that sense oncoming obstacles and automatically apply the brakes faster than a human driver can react. A few cars even feature parking assist technology that intelligently steers a car into a parking space. GPS and mapping technology have made it possible for drivers not only to determine where they are but also to find the most efficient route to a given destination. To create a truly self-driving car, all of these systems and more must be integrated into a single vehicle.

The key to making all of those systems work together is the use of electronic control units (ECUs). These systems control the electronic functions of a car. They handle everything from automatic braking to closing the trunk. Today's cars must process many streams of information at once. Modern cars may have dozens of separate ECUs coordinating their systems. Electrical engineers are responsible for developing these systems and understanding how they will work together to make the car safe for drivers. As Bruce Emaus, a computer expert with the Society of Automotive Engineers, puts it, "It would be easy to say the modern car is a computer on wheels, but it's more like 30 or more computers on wheels."[1]

In one driverless car developed at Stanford University, the electronic equipment controlling the vehicle is located in the trunk.

STEERING TOWARD PROGRESS

The engineers working on the Google driverless cars have taken existing automotive computer technology and gone several steps further. Their goal is to completely replace the human driver with a computer one. Incredible progress has already been made.

The Google car begins its journey when a passenger enters the vehicle and gives the car the address of his or her destination. The computer system uses Google's own mapping software to locate the address. The car then uses an array of sensors to keep it on track during its journey. The rotating lidar, or light radar, sensor on the roof can scan more than 200 feet (60 m) in every direction and create a three-dimensional map of the car's immediate surroundings. A position estimator located on the left rear wheel helps the car keep track of its position on the destination map. Three radar sensors spread evenly across the front bumper, along with one on the rear bumper, detect the car's position with respect to other cars on the road. A forward-facing video camera located near the rearview mirror informs the computer of obstacles in its direct path.

The brain of the Google driverless car sits in the trunk. It is a computer attached to the vehicle's many sensors. As Chris Urmson, a leader on Google's driverless car project, explains, "The car is constantly checking hundreds of variables."[2] The computer brain of the Google car processes

CHRIS URMSON

Chris Urmson is on the team developing Google's self-driving car technology. He earned his PhD in 2005 from Carnegie Mellon University and his bachelor's degree in computer engineering from the University of Manitoba in 1998.

In 2007, Urmson was the director of technology for a team that won that year's DARPA challenge. DARPA, the Defense Advanced Research Projects Agency, is a government group that works to advance cutting-edge technology. Its DARPA Grand Challenge competitions motivate engineers to move forward in the field of autonomous vehicles. In 2007, the goal was to build an autonomous car capable of navigating traffic, merging, passing, stopping, and eventually parking safely.

Urmson has been a member of the Robotics Institute at Carnegie Mellon since 1998. In this position, he has helped develop many robot vehicles. Boss was the name of the autonomous car that won the 2007 DARPA challenge. Urmson believes that "self-driving vehicles hold the promise of transforming the automotive industry and reshaping our relationship with the automobile."[3]

Urmson's car, Boss, featured bulkier sensors than those found on the latest versions of Google's car.

the information it receives and decides how the car should react to its environment. It sends electric signals to the devices that operate steering, braking, and accelerating mechanisms.

Lead engineer Sebastian Thrun believes autonomous cars are the wave of the future. He thinks they will decrease overall car usage, save the environment from pollution, and increase safety for travelers, among other benefits:

> If the car could drive itself, you could be much safer, and you could achieve something during your commute. You can also envision a futuristic society in which we share cars much better. Cars could come to you when you need them; you wouldn't have to have private car ownership, which means no need for a garage, no need for a driveway, no need for your workplace to have as many parking spots.[4]

CHAPTER 8

IMPROVING THE DRIVERLESS CAR

The engineers behind the Google driverless car did not simply sit down and create it. It was the product of years of research and development. Much of this development stemmed from an organization in the US Department of Defense called the Defense Advanced Research Projects Agency (DARPA). In 2004, DARPA sought to stimulate progress in the field of robotic cars. It challenged engineers across the country to create a robot-driven vehicle capable of traveling 150 miles (240 km) across the Mojave Desert in one day. It offered a $1 million prize for winning the competition. Not one of the 13 robots that started the race was able to complete the challenge. The top

The first DARPA race attracted teams with robot vehicles of many shapes and sizes.

performer traveled only 7.4 miles (11.9 km).[1] Another challenge was scheduled for the next year. The engineers quickly learned from their mistakes. In 2005, five robots crossed the finish line.

Many of the engineers on the Google driverless car project were first introduced to autonomous cars when they tried to construct one for the DARPA contest. Chris Urmson's team from Carnegie Mellon University successfully completed the 2007 DARPA challenge. He is now one of the lead engineers on the Google driverless car project.

DRIVING LIKE A PRO

The Google driverless car has performed exceedingly well in its test drives. It has demonstrated it can smoothly merge into moving traffic, maintain proper distances between cars, and even make sudden adjustments when a car in front of it unexpectedly stops. Urmson explains the car's capabilities: "This car can do 75 miles per hour [121 kmh]. It can track pedestrians and cyclists. It understands traffic lights. It can merge at highway speeds."[2]

The computer monitor on the passenger-side dashboard of the car shows everything in its view. Using its lidar technology, the computer processes the location of the lanes while keeping track of the speed and

distance of other cars. The computer uses algorithms that can predict where each object will be in the future. The computer acquires each object as a target and tracks its progress with red boxes and tracer lines. Google's Anthony Levandowski says, "We're analyzing and predicting the world 20 times a second."[3]

When another car accelerates up the merge lane, the Google car must make the same decision a human driver would. Does it accelerate to get in front of the approaching car or slow down to allow the car to merge in front of it? Even after the Google car makes a decision, it is capable of changing its mind if the merging car decelerates to come in behind it. So far, the Google cars have performed extremely well in situations like this.

DISTRACTION-FREE DRIVING

As Google sees it, the safety offered by its driverless cars is its biggest benefit. Sebastian Thrun says, "According to the World Health Organization, more than 1.2 million lives are

THE PRICE OF AUTONOMY

Each Google driverless car possesses approximately $150,000 in computer equipment, as well as a lidar system that costs approximately $70,000.[4] The price of the sophisticated but necessary equipment must come down significantly for these cars to be cost-effective for mass production.

lost every year in road traffic accidents. We believe our technology has the potential to cut that number, perhaps by as much as half."[5] Google's claim is that a robotic car is focused solely on driving, preventing one of the biggest issues with human drivers: distractions. Statistics in the United States confirm Google's view. John Maddox with the National Highway

Futuristic concepts of driverless cars suggest the problem of distracted driving will someday become a thing of the past.

RESPONSIBILITY FOR CRASHES

Advocates for the driverless car are worried about one thing the car cannot control—liability in accidents. Who is liable if a driverless car is involved in an accident? Liability now is based on who is blamed for the accident. If the driver is the computer designed by the car's manufacturer, would the law hold the manufacturer responsible? If a person responsible for an accident would have gone to jail, what would happen to the responsible party in an accident involving a driverless car? Questions like this must be answered before driverless cars enter widespread use.

Traffic Safety Administration states, "Human error is the critical reason for 93 percent of crashes."[6]

Google's driverless cars have been nearly accident-free. In 2011, one of the cars rear-ended another car near the Google headquarters. But the human driver was to blame, since the car was not in self-driving mode at the time. The incident does raise an important question, though. If it is the robot's fault, who receives the blame for an accident involving a driverless car? The question is important to drivers, governments, and insurance companies alike. The answer will have a huge impact on how driverless cars are eventually accepted into society.

ROUGH PATCHES

Besides raising issues about liability, Google driverless cars also face other performance challenges that must be resolved before they can be fully integrated onto the roadways. One of the biggest concerns is that Google cars have a hard time driving in adverse weather conditions such as rain, ice, and snow. The sensors cannot see the lanes of the road well when snow or rain is falling. Urmson says this is "because the appearance and shape of the world changes. It can't figure out where to go or what to do."[7]

Engineers designed the car's navigation system to rely heavily on preprogrammed map information. Before a driverless car sets out, every inch of road, the traffic signals and signs, and all intersections are mapped and the data is uploaded to the control system. If a route or roadway does not appear on the map, it does not exist for the car. This means the car, like humans, can get lost if changes have been made to roadways or routes. Google cars also do not understand how to handle the presence of stalled vehicles on the side of the road, construction zones, or accidents

ROBOT DRIVING BREAKTHROUGH

Car manufacturer Toyota is working on a system it calls Automated Highway Driving Assist (AHDA). It will use a combination of automated driving technologies to support safer driving on highways. AHDA will link two existing technologies, cooperative-adaptive cruise control and lane trace control. The idea is to help the driver maintain a proper speed and distance in the lanes between cars by communicating with surrounding cars. Toyota has built its first prototype and hopes to have the cars ready in the next few years for production.

Mechanics often use computers to diagnose car problems. Hackers can use the same systems to interfere with the operation of many modern cars.

involving other cars. Engineers are working on new algorithms to allow the computer systems to deal with these.

COMPUTER HACKERS

The computers in an autonomous car, as with any computers, are susceptible to threats from outsiders. Car hacking is a term used to describe unauthorized access to a car's computers. It can be done directly when the hacker plugs into a car, or remotely if the car is connected to the Internet or another computer network. It is a genuine threat to today's automobiles. The military has researched how easy it is to hack into a car's computer system and gain control of it. In a test, two government-funded hackers, Charlie Miller and Chris Valasek, were able to use a laptop to take control of the computer systems of a Toyota Prius and a Ford Escape. Miller and Valasek say the danger of car hacking is scary because "drivers and passengers are strictly at the mercy of the code running in their automobiles and, unlike when their web browser crashes or is compromised, the threat to their physical well-being is real."[8]

Google engineers continue to devise new algorithms, optimize sensors, and improve the devices that control the operation of their driverless car. They hope within a few decades autonomous cars will be transporting drivers safely and dependably from one place to another.

CHAPTER 9

ENGINEERING THE FUTURE

Electrical engineers are at the forefront of many groundbreaking areas of science and technology. Today, many new projects are challenging engineers to develop breakthroughs that will make electronic devices cheaper, more efficient, better for the environment, and safer to use.

One such project is led by Srdjan Lukic, assistant professor of electrical engineering at North Carolina State University. His team is developing a way to transfer energy wirelessly from a stationary source to an object moving past it. Their goal is to create stations that can

Electrical engineers are studying ways of powering vehicles, including buses, by wirelessly transmitting electricity.

recharge electric cars while they are driving through. Charging electric cars usually involves plugging the car into a charging station. Relatively few of these stations exist, and the charging process can take hours. Developing these small drive-through chargers will help improve the range of electric cars, one of the key challenges the vehicles face in achieving widespread popularity. The researchers created a way for energy to flow between two circuits without them physically touching each other. A series of transmitter coils in the charger gives off an electromagnetic field. A car is then outfitted with a receiver coil.

The key to this invention is the ability of the receiver to wirelessly connect with the transmitter coil as it passes by. When the transmitter coil senses the receiver coil, it automatically increases its current. This boosts the magnetic field strength and speeds the energy transfer. The receiver accepts the electricity and funnels it into the battery of the car. After the car has passed, the current on the transmitter coil returns to normal levels. Lukic and his colleagues have developed a small functional prototype of their model and are working to create a larger-scale system.

COOLING THE EFFECT OF THE SUN'S RAYS

Electrical engineers at Stanford University have created a new type of radiative panel that can be attached to buildings to keep them cool during

Transferring electricity from place to place without wires may lead to exciting breakthroughs in many products and fields.

the hottest part of the day. As Shanhui Fan, a professor of electrical engineering at the institution, explains, "People usually see space as a source of heat from the sun, but away from the sun outer space is really

The driverless car pods at Heathrow Airport
have completely replaced the bus system
at the terminal where they are used.

a cold, cold place."[1] The sun only heats things up when its light strikes them. The researchers have managed to minimize the sun's heating effects by creating panels that reflect both sunlight and heat back into the atmosphere.

This is a difficult task. Even mirrors absorb a large portion of sunlight, causing them to heat up. The heat they generate would be transferred to the building where they reside. Stanford's new panels reflect the majority of sunlight at a specific wavelength. This allows it to escape Earth's atmosphere instead of being reflected back to the ground.

The potential for these new cooling panels is enormous. Covering 10 percent of a home's roof with them could lower summertime air conditioning needs by 35 percent.[2] Multiplied over many buildings in many cities, that adds up to huge economic savings. Professor Fan sees worldwide applications for the radiative cooling panels, especially in countries where air conditioning is not affordable or feasible.

DRIVERLESS CAR PODS

Engineers are creating exciting improvements in the area of transportation as well. Besides Google's driverless car program, other groups are making

advances in public transit systems. Electrical engineers in the United Kingdom have created driverless car pods used at Heathrow Airport in London. The pods are constructed like miniature subway cars and can hold four passengers comfortably.

The cars are electrically powered, using batteries specially designed to provide maximum output while still being small and light. They provide energy to propel the vehicle along a track atop four rubber tires. The control system of the pod manages the timing between each pod, ensuring no two pods collide. The system dispatches a pod when a customer requests one. Each pod is equipped with a laser system that continually verifies position, direction, and speed to keep the pod on track.

The pods are already in use in Heathrow Airport, but the United Kingdom is preparing for trials to bring the pods to Milton Keynes, a large town in Buckinghamshire. A track for the pods is being constructed between Milton Keynes's train station and shopping center. Planners expect it to be completed in 2015. If all goes well, the engineers hope to eventually remove the rails and have the pods operate on sidewalks. The idea is that people will call for pods via their smartphones and have autonomous rides to wherever they wish to go.

THE NEED FOR ELECTRICAL ENGINEERS

Michael Buryk of the Institute of Electrical and Electronics Engineers says the need for electrical engineers is great: "Electrical engineers, especially those who work as power engineers, are in short supply."[3] The rapid growth of alternative energy technology means engineers will be needed to build the power plants and power grids of the future.

POWERING THE FUTURE

One of the biggest challenges for electrical engineers today is creating new, more efficient batteries. With the advent of handheld and wearable devices, such as smartphones, tablets, and fitness bands and watches, the need for tiny but powerful batteries is increasing. The small size of these gadgets and their constant use require efficient, compact power sources. The size of the battery is not the only limitation for use in a wearable device. Some of the gadgets, such as wristbands or watches, are curved for better fit around the wrist. Engineers have developed curved batteries that fit snugly inside these devices. A goal of battery research is to make it possible for users to wear these tiny devices for days at a time without having to take them off and recharge them.

The technological problems we face today represent opportunities for the electrical engineers of the future.

Electrical engineering once consisted mainly of power generation and the study of electricity. As technology advanced rapidly in the 1900s, the field has branched out to include a vast array of scientific and technical areas. An electrical engineer could end up working with satellites in orbit around Earth, innovative new renewable sources of energy, or self-driving cars. University professors are involving their students in research that is making great strides in the field. New electrical engineers are learning to apply their skills in innovative ways. The career path for electrical engineers is wide open and encompasses many fields. As Cornell University tells its electrical engineering and computer engineering students, "Electrical engineers can do anything!"[4]

HANDS-ON PROJECT
THINKING ABOUT DRIVERLESS CARS

Self-driving cars are one of the most challenging projects electrical engineers are working on today. Although Google has made great progress, there is still a long way to go before the cars can enter widespread use. As with any project, the first task of engineers is to identify the problems that need to be solved.

The next time you take a ride in a car, bring along a notebook and pen. Observing the car, the driver, and the surroundings, write down all of the problems you can think of that would need to be solved before a fully self-driving car can be created. For example, how does the driver's behavior change depending on the weather? Does she drive differently if it is cold, rainy, or windy? Next, think of how you could solve these

People are still determining how society and the law will treat driverless cars compared to ordinary cars.

problems. What kinds of sensors and control systems could a self-driving car use to behave in the same way?

Then, think of the ways in which a human driver has different needs than a robot driver. For instance, a human driver needs to be able to see through the windshield. He or she must scrape ice off it in winter. Would this be necessary for a robot driver? Are there any factors that would affect robot drivers but not human drivers?

Once you have collected a list of problems, potential solutions, and differences between robot and human drivers, search the Internet for more information about driverless car programs and answer the following questions:

- Is there any overlap between the problems you identified and the problems identified by engineers working on driverless cars today? If so, how did your solutions compare with those under development by the engineers?

- Based on your thought experiment and the information you read, what are the pros and cons of driverless cars versus human drivers?

- When driverless cars eventually reach the public, would you ride in them? Why or why not?

PLANNING A CAREER

Future electrical engineers should take high school courses in algebra, trigonometry, calculus, and physics. In addition, courses in computer hardware and software are helpful due to the relationship between electrical and computer engineering.

↓

Entry-level electrical engineering jobs usually require a bachelor's degree, which means four years of study at a college or university. In the electrical engineering major, courses may cover advanced math, control systems, and electric circuits. Students often work in laboratories and do hands-on training.

↓

Many engineers go on to receive their master's degree and even a PhD in an engineering specialty.

ESSENTIAL FACTS
GLOBAL POSITIONING SYSTEM

PROJECT DATES
The NTS-2 satellite first tested the GPS concept in 1977. The system is still in use today.

KEY PLAYERS
The work of physicist Albert Einstein led to the precise timing calculations needed for GPS. Roger Easton contributed spacecraft tracking and timing technology. Karen VanDyke helped develop a system to make GPS more useful for pilots.

KEY TOOLS AND TECHNOLOGIES
- A constellation of satellites orbits Earth at specific altitudes and transmits time and location data to ground-based monitoring stations and millions of handheld devices.

- Consumer GPS devices pick up the faint signals from the satellites and use them to determine their location on the planet.

THE IMPACT OF THE GLOBAL POSITIONING SYSTEM
The precise location data provided by GPS has applications for the military, pilots, boaters, and everyday consumers. The system's timing data is used by corporations to keep precise chronological records.

ESSENTIAL FACTS
NELLIS AIR FORCE BASE SOLAR PLANT

PROJECT DATES
Construction began in April 2007 and ended in December of that year. The plant officially opened on December 17.

KEY PLAYERS
Nellis AFB hosts the solar power plant, which was designed and built by SunPower Corporation. Nevada Power, the local power utility, connected the plant to its power grid.

KEY TOOLS AND TECHNOLOGIES
- The plant's photovoltaic cells and panels feature innovative designs that boost their efficiency.
- An advanced tracking system keeps the panels facing the sun throughout the day.

THE IMPACT OF THE NELLIS AFB SOLAR PLANT
The power plant meets approximately one-quarter of the base's electricity requirements and saves an estimated $1 million per year in energy costs. The use of renewable energy cuts the amount of pollution generated by the base's operations.

ESSENTIAL FACTS
GOOGLE DRIVERLESS CAR

PROJECT DATES
The project was announced to the public in 2010. Google continues to refine its driverless car technology.

KEY PLAYERS
Sebastian Thrun, a professor of computer science and electrical engineering at Stanford University, led the development of the car. Chris Urmson led a team that won the DARPA challenge and is a robotics expert involved in the Google project. Anthony Levandowski is another lead engineer on the project.

KEY TOOLS AND TECHNOLOGIES
- The Google driverless car uses precise sensors to observe its surroundings.
- Specialized computers analyze the sensor data and take appropriate action to control the car in response.

THE IMPACT OF THE GOOGLE DRIVERLESS CAR
The impact of widespread driverless cars will be enormous. Fatal accidents could be dramatically reduced due to the removal of the potential for human error. Cars that take the most efficient possible routes will also save more fuel.

GLOSSARY

actuator
A mechanical device that converts energy into motion.

algorithm
A step-by-step procedure for solving a mathematical problem in a limited number of steps.

attitude control
The ability to change the orientation of an object.

autonomous
Not controlled by outside forces.

dynamo
An electric generator that produces direct current.

electronic control unit
Any embedded system that controls electric systems in a car.

grid connected
A power generating system connected directly to the utility grid.

lidar
A remote sensing technology that measures distance by illuminating a target with a laser and analyzing the reflected light.

load
A device that receives electric power.

organic molecule
A molecule that contains carbon atoms and that is typically associated with living things.

photovoltaic cell
A device that converts the energy of light into electricity.

radiative
Able to send out in waves.

solar array
A group of solar panels interconnected to form a large power source.

ADDITIONAL RESOURCES

SELECTED BIBLIOGRAPHY

GPS.gov. US Government, 2014. Web.

Hoffman, Jane, and Michael Hoffman. *Green: Your Place in the New Energy Revolution*. New York: Palgrave, 2008. Print.

"Solar Energy Basics." *National Renewable Energy Laboratory*. US Government, 2012. Web.

FURTHER READINGS

Gibilisco, Stan. *Electricity Demystified*. New York: McGraw-Hill, 2012. Print.

Zuchora-Walske, Christine. *Solar Energy*. Minneapolis, MN: Abdo, 2013. Print.

WEBSITES

To learn more about Great Achievements in Engineering, visit **booklinks.abdopublishing.com**. These links are routinely monitored and updated to provide the most current information available.

FOR MORE INFORMATION

For more information on this subject, contact or visit the following organizations:

Hans Flat Solar Array

Canyonlands National Park

2282 SW Resource Blvd.

Moab, UT 84532

435-719-2100

http://www.nps.gov/cany/planyourvisit/mazesolarpower.htm

The solar power plant at Nellis Air Force Base is not easy to see up close, but this smaller solar installation at a national park in Utah is open to the public. The panels share some features in common with the Nellis panels, including a tracking system.

Museum of Science and Industry

5700 S. Lake Shore Drive

Chicago, IL 60637

773-684-1414

http://www.msichicago.org

This enormous museum features exhibits on science and technology, including many objects and systems developed by electrical engineers.

SOURCE NOTES

CHAPTER 1. LICENSED TO DRIVE

1. "What We're Driving At." *Google Official Blog*. Google, 9 Oct. 2010. Web. 1 Apr. 2014.

2. Henry Fountain. "Yes, Driverless Cars Know the Way to San Jose." *New York Times*. New York Times, 26 Oct. 2012. Web. 1 Apr. 2014.

3. Ibid.

4. John Markoff. "Google Cars Drive Themselves, in Traffic." *New York Times*. New York Times, 9 Oct. 2010. Web. 2 Dec. 2013.

5. Josh Grasmick. "The Auto Industry's $2 Trillion Breakthrough: Driverless Cars." *Money Morning*. Money Morning, 3 Oct. 2013. Web. 1 Apr. 2014.

6. "Electrical Engineers." *Occupational Employment Statistics*. Bureau of Labor Statistics, May 2013. Web. 1 Apr. 2014.

7. Aaron Smith. "Top-Paying Jobs Are in Engineering." *CNN*. CNN, 25 Apr. 2013. Web. 1 Apr. 2014.

CHAPTER 2. ELECTRICAL ENGINEERING

1. "MIT EECS Department Facts." *MIT*. MIT, n.d. Web. 16 Dec. 2013.

CHAPTER 3. CREATING GPS

1. "Space Segment." *GPS.gov*. GPS.gov, 1 Apr. 2014. Web. 1 Apr. 2014.

CHAPTER 4. GPS IN ACTION

1. "Tick-Tock Atomic Clock." *NASA Science News*. NASA, 8 Apr. 2002. Web. 1 Apr. 2014.

2. Joe Mueller. "GPS Tracking Jammers: Problems and Uses." *GPS for Today*. GPS for Today, 25 Feb. 2010. Web. 1 Apr. 2014.

3. "Consumer Alert: Using or Importing Jammers is Illegal." *FCC*. FCC, 6 Mar. 2012. Web. 1 Apr. 2014.

4. Melody Ward Leslie. "Karen VanDyke: Re-Engineering the Airways." *Inside GNSS*. Inside GNSS, June 2006. Web. 1 Apr. 2014.

CHAPTER 5. HARNESSING THE SUN'S ENERGY

1. "Nellis Air Force Base Solar Power System." *Nellis Air Force Base*. US Air Force, n.d. Web. 9 Apr. 2014.

2. Ibid.

3. "Top 6 Things You Didn't Know about Solar Energy." *Energy.gov*. Energy. gov, 6 June 2012. Web. 23 Dec. 2013.

4. "T20 Single Axis Solar Tracker." *SunPower*. SunPower, 2014. Web. 9 Apr. 2014.

5. "National Solar Job Census 2012." *Solar Foundation*. Solar Foundation, n.d. Web. 9 Apr. 2014.

CHAPTER 6. SOLAR CHALLENGES

1. Annie Snider. "Defense: Clean Energy Doesn't Always Bring Security for Military." *E&E Publishing*. E&E Publishing, 27 Jan. 2012. Web. 9 Apr. 2014.

2. Tom Murphy. "Don't Be a PV Efficiency Snob." *Do the Math*. University of California San Diego, 21 Sept. 2011. Web. 9 Apr. 2014.

3. "Most Efficient Solar." *SunPower*. SunPower, 2014. Web. 9 Apr. 2014.

4. Cory Nealon. "Solar Panels as Inexpensive as Paint?" *Science Daily*. Science Daily, 13 May 2013. Web. 22 Dec. 2013.

5. "Nellis Air Force Base Solar Array Provides Model for Renewable Projects." *Energy.gov*. Energy.gov, 24 Mar. 2010. Web. 9 Apr. 2014.

6. "Nellis Air Force Base Solar Power System." *Nellis Air Force Base*. US Air Force, n.d. Web. 9 Apr. 2014.

7. "Nellis Air Force Base Saves over $1,000,000 a Year on Energy Costs." *SunPower*. SunPower, Dec. 2007. Web. 9 Apr. 2014.

SOURCE NOTES CONTINUED

CHAPTER 7. A ROBOT DRIVER

1. Jim Motavalli. "The Dozens of Computers That Make Modern Cars Go (and Stop)." *New York Times*. New York Times, 4 Feb. 2010. Web. 26 Dec. 2013.

2. "Notes from the Driverless Car Summit." *Motor Trend*. Motor Trend, Sept. 2012. Web. 9 Apr. 2014.

3. Chris Urmson. "The Google Self-Driving Car Project." *Robotics Science and Systems*. University of Southern California, n.d. Web. 9 Apr. 2014.

4. Sebastian Thrun. "Google's Original X-Man: A Conversation With Sebastian Thrun." *Foreign Affairs*. Foreign Affairs, Nov./Dec. 2013. Web. 9 Apr. 2014.

CHAPTER 8. IMPROVING THE DRIVERLESS CAR

1. "Desert Race Too Tough for Robots." *BBC News*. BBC, 15 Mar. 2004. Web. 9 Apr. 2014.

2. Tom Vanderbilt. "Let the Robot Drive: The Autonomous Car of the Future Is Here." *Wired*. Wired, 20 Jan. 2012. Web. 27 Dec. 2013.

3. Ibid.

4. Alisa Priddle and Chris Woodyard. "Google Discloses Costs of Its Driverless Car Tests." *USA Today*. USA Today, 14 June 2012. Web. 9 Apr. 2014.

5. "What We're Driving At." *Google Blog*. Google, 9 Oct. 2010. Web. 2 Dec. 2013.

6. James M. Flammang. "Era of Driverless Cars May Be Near, Ideally Reducing Crashes and Fatalities." *AutoMedia.com*. AutoMedia.com, 7 July 2012. Web. 9 Apr. 2014.

7. Joann Muller. "No Hands, No Feet: My Unnerving Ride in Google's Driverless Car." *Forbes*. Forbes, 21 Mar. 2013. Web. 9 Apr. 2014.

8. Holly Ellyat. "Car Hacking: The Next Global Cybercrime?" *CNBC*. CNBC, 18 Oct. 2013. Web. 27 Dec. 2013.

CHAPTER 9. ENGINEERING THE FUTURE

1. Andrew Myers. "Stanford Scientists Develop New Type of Solar Structure That Cools Buildings in Full Sunlight." *Stanford News*. Stanford University, 15 Apr. 2013. Web. 27 Dec. 2013.

2. Ibid.

3. "The 12 Best Engineering and Information Technology Jobs." *CareerCast.com*. CareerCast.com, n.d. Web. 9 Apr. 2014.

4. "Message from Cornell ECE's Associate Director." *School of Electrical and Computer Engineering*. Cornell University, 2014. Web. 9 Apr. 2014.

INDEX

ABOUT THE AUTHOR

Jennifer Swanson is the author of more than 16 nonfiction books for kids. She has a bachelor's degree in chemistry and a master's degree in K–8 science. She took a year of electrical engineering in her undergraduate program at the US Naval Academy and enjoyed working in the lab creating circuits.